TRUE OR *FALSE?*

PENICILLIN
WAS DISCOVERED
BY ACCIDENT

And Other Facts About Inventions and Discoveries

JAN PAYNE AND STEVEN WILDER

Enslow Publishing
101 W. 23rd Street
Suite 240
New York, NY 10011
USA

enslow.com

Published in 2017 by Enslow Publishing, LLC.
101 W. 23rd Street, Suite 240, New York, NY 10011

Published in 2017 by Enslow Publishing, LLC, by permission of the Reader's Digest Association Inc., 44 South Broadway, White Plains, New York, 10601

Library of Congress Cataloging-in-Publication Data
Names: Payne, Jan. | Wilder, Steven.
Title: Penicillin was discovered by accident : and other facts about inventions and discoveries / Jan Payne and Steven Wilder.
Description: New York, NY : Enslow Publishing, 2017. | Series: True or false? | Audience: Age 8-up. | Audience: Grade 4 to 6. | Includes bibliographical references and index.
Identifiers: LCCN 2016005253| ISBN 9780766077423 (library bound) | ISBN 9780766077393 (pbk.) | ISBN 9780766077409 (6-pack)
Subjects: LCSH: Inventions--History--Juvenile literature. | Technology--History--Juvenile literature.
Classification: LCC T48 .P39 2017 | DDC 609--dc23
LC record available at http://lccn.loc.gov/2016005253

Printed in the United States of America

To Our Readers: We have done our best to make sure all website addresses in this book were active and appropriate when we went to press. However, the author and the publisher have no control over and assume no liability for the material available on those websites or on any websites they may link to. Any comments or suggestions can be sent by e-mail to customerservice@enslow.com.

Cover illustration by Joel R. Gennari

Interior illustrations by Paul Moran

Photo credits: maodoltee/Shutterstock.com (backgrounds throughout book); Nobelus/Shutterstock.com (dingbat on spine).

CONTENTS

Introduction

Did you know the first bicycle had no pedals? That scientists have reproduced the big bang in a lab? Or that medieval barbers performed surgery? Or did they? This book is full of fascinating facts and fat fibs—and it's up to you to decipher which is which.

From facts about historical figures, events, and even creatures, you will have a great time testing your knowledge, while learning some astonishing truths and uncovering some large lies along the way. Then check out the shocking facts that follow to see if your lie-detecting skills are up to snuff.

IT'S UP TO YOU

Here's how it works. Each section contains a list of facts. On a separate sheet of paper, mark your answers to each "fact." Then turn to page 44 to see if you're a science supreme!

So what are you waiting for? Grab a pencil and some paper and see if you can spot the twisted truths. Why not test your family and friends to see if they know the facts? You never know! You may surprise them with some of the stranger-than-fiction truths waiting to amaze you on these fun-packed pages.

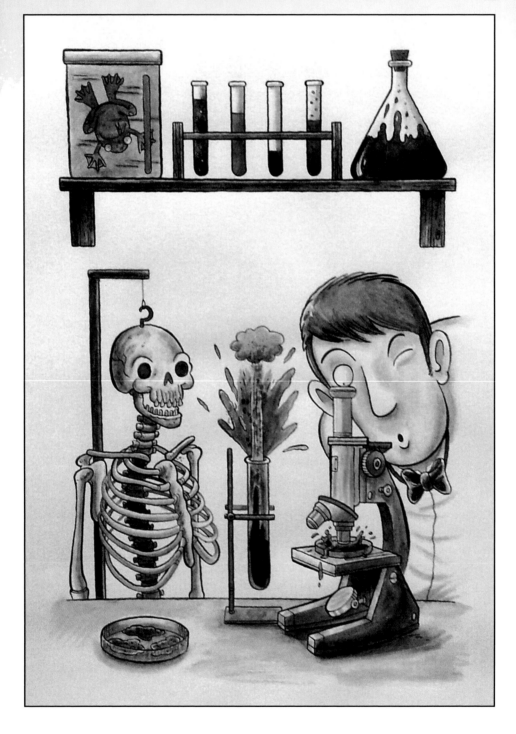

TERRIFIC TECHNOLOGY

QUIZ

Humans have been toying with technology for centuries—from the first tools used by cave dwellers to the latest gadgets. Decide whether the following facts are technologically true or fundamentally false. Keep track of your answers on a separate sheet of paper.

THE "FACTS"

	TRUE	FALSE
1. The first bicycle had no pedals.	☐	☐
2. The first "mobile" phones were too heavy to carry around.	☐	☐
3. The screen on the first television set was more than 78 inches (2 m) wide.	☐	☐
4. The first flush toilet was invented by Thomas Crapper in 1861.	☐	☐
5. It took eight hours to take the world's first photograph.	☐	☐
6. The world's fastest train floats above the tracks.	☐	☐
7. The first helicopter design was sketched by Leonardo da Vinci in the 15th century.	☐	☐

1. THE FIRST BICYCLE HAD NO PEDALS.

TRUE

One of the first bicycles was invented in 1790. It was made from wood but had no steering or pedals. The rider sat astride it and moved by pushing their feet along the ground. In 1817 Karl Drais improved it with his "running bicycle," which could be steered. A blacksmith named Kirkpatrick MacMillan added pedals in 1839. The design was further improved later that century by the addition of a chain and pneumatic (air-filled) tires, which led to the bicycle becoming safer and very popular.

2. THE FIRST "MOBILE" PHONES WERE TOO HEAVY TO CARRY AROUND.

TRUE

The first mobile phone call was made in 1973, but it was almost a decade before the first handsets went on sale. Early handsets looked like a phone stuck on a car battery. They were very heavy and had a talk time of just 20 minutes. In 1983 the "brick" handset was launched. It got its name because it was as big as a brick and only a little lighter. It cost so much that few people could afford it.

3. THE SCREEN ON THE FIRST TELEVISION SET WAS MORE THAN 78 INCHES (2 M) WIDE.

FALSE

John Logie Baird first demonstrated his "televisor" machine in 1926. The screen was not huge. In fact, it was so small that only one person could see the picture at a time, and the image was very weak. At that point, sound could not be transmitted at the same time as the picture.

4. THE FIRST FLUSH TOILET WAS INVENTED BY THOMAS CRAPPER IN 1861.

FALSE

Many people wrongly believe that a man named Thomas Crapper invented the flush toilet. In fact, its design has been refined over centuries by numerous people. Toilets with a very simple flush system have been found in the ruins of the palace at Knossos, Crete—dating from 4,000 years ago! In 1596 Sir John Harrington built one for Queen Elizabeth I of England. The waste was flushed away through a trapdoor that opened directly into a cesspool. The smell was so awful that it didn't catch on. In 1820 Albert Giblin patented his design for the flush toilet, but it was 37 years before the first toilet paper was sold to go with it!

5. IT TOOK EIGHT HOURS TO TAKE THE WORLD'S FIRST PHOTOGRAPH.

TRUE

When Joseph Niépce took the world's first photograph in 1826, it wasn't just a case of "point and shoot," as it is with today's digital cameras. It was a complex process involving a pewter plate coated with chemicals. This was placed in something called a "camera obscura." Light was projected onto a flat surface inside the camera, producing an image of the scene outside. It took eight hours for light to harden the chemicals on the plate. The plate was then washed in more chemicals to reveal the image. Further developments saw a move from plates to film, then to the digital process that is used by cameras today.

6. THE WORLD'S FASTEST TRAIN FLOATS ABOVE THE TRACKS.

TRUE

China's Maglev train (the name comes from "magnetic levitation") floats 0.4 inches (1 cm) above the tracks, thanks to electromagnets in the train and tracks. It travels at speeds of up to 267 miles (430 km) per hour.

7. THE FIRST HELICOPTER DESIGN WAS SKETCHED BY LEONARDO DA VINCI IN THE 15TH CENTURY.

TRUE

Leonardo da Vinci was what's known as a Renaissance man, which means that he was interested in everything and was good at most things. He is probably best known as the 15th-century artist who painted the Mona Lisa, but the sketches and notebooks he left behind are equally important. Among his sketches are early designs for a helicopter and scuba gear, although it was several centuries before the ideas became reality.

Chapter Two

DRAMATIC DISCOVERIES

QUIZ

Throughout history, dramatic discoveries have been made, and some of them seemed quite shocking at the time. Can you determine which discoveries are terrific truths and which are tall tales? Keep score on a separate sheet of paper.

THE "FACTS"

	TRUE	FALSE
1. Sir Isaac Newton wrote his theory on the law of gravity after an apple fell on his head.	☐	☐
2. Fire has been used by humans for more than a million years.	☐	☐
3. Watching icebergs led to the theory of continental drift.	☐	☐
4. Michael Faraday discovered electricity in 1831.	☐	☐
5. Galileo was arrested and his books banned when he claimed that the Earth revolved around the sun.	☐	☐
6. Charles Darwin's ideas in his book *On the Origin of Species* were so radical that he delayed publishing them for years.	☐	☐

1. SIR ISAAC NEWTON WROTE HIS THEORY ON THE LAW OF GRAVITY AFTER AN APPLE FELL ON HIS HEAD.

FALSE

Sir Isaac Newton was one of Britain's most influential scientists. He wrote his theory on the law of gravity in the 17th century, but it doesn't mention an apple hitting him on the head. It's more likely that he had seen one falling from a tree and later anecdotes were embellished to jazz the story up.

2. FIRE HAS BEEN USED BY HUMANS FOR MORE THAN A MILLION YEARS.

TRUE

Early humans started to use fires that occurred naturally—as a result of lightning strikes or the friction of rock falls—more than 1.5 million years ago. It took a long time before they discovered how to make it. When they found a fire that had started naturally, they would keep the fire going and use it for warmth and food. About 10,000 years ago people discovered how to make fire by striking a flint against a rock called pyrite.

3. WATCHING ICEBERGS LED TO THE THEORY OF CONTINENTAL DRIFT.

TRUE

In 1912 Alfred Wegener noticed that on a map, the east coast of South America looked as if it fit into the west coast of Africa, like a jigsaw puzzle. Then one day he was watching icebergs drifting out to sea and realized that the continents must be moving, too. It was not until the 1960s that scientists could prove his theory.

4. MICHAEL FARADAY DISCOVERED ELECTRICITY IN 1831.

FALSE

People were aware of electricity even in ancient times. But until a man named Faraday discovered that magnetism could produce electricity, which is known as electromagnetic induction, it was considered to be nothing more than a curiosity. Faraday went on to develop an electric motor and generator. His findings made it possible to harness electricity as power for the first time.

5. GALILEO WAS ARRESTED AND HIS BOOKS BANNED WHEN HE CLAIMED THAT THE EARTH REVOLVED AROUND THE SUN.

TRUE

Galileo Galilei was a 17th-century Italian astronomer and philosopher who used one of the first telescopes to study the universe. His discoveries supported earlier claims by a man named Copernicus, who believed the planets revolved around the sun. This was seen as a

challenge to the Catholic Church, because at the time, the church believed that everything revolved around the Earth. Galileo's claims led to him being tried and found guilty of heresy—which means disagreeing with the beliefs and teachings of the Catholic Church. Galileo was kept under house arrest for the rest of his life.

6. CHARLES DARWIN'S IDEAS IN HIS BOOK *ON THE ORIGIN OF SPECIES* WERE SO RADICAL THAT HE DELAYED PUBLISHING THEM FOR YEARS.

TRUE

A scientist named Charles Darwin spent many years on an expedition to study plants and animals. He observed that creatures have to compete with each other for food and shelter. Within each species, certain creatures were born with features that made them more able to survive than others and pass the features on to their young. Over time these features became more common, so the species changed, or "evolved." For example, a moth that was darker than others blended better with dark tree bark. As a result, it was less likely to be eaten by birds and therefore more likely to survive and pass on its darker shade. At this time, many people believed that the world was created by God in seven days. Darwin's ideas were so radical that he spent more than 20 years carefully gathering evidence before he published his theory of "natural selection" in 1859. As he expected, when his ideas were finally published, many people were outraged.

Chapter Three

WEIRD SCIENCE

QUIZ

Brilliant as they are, some scientific experiments and discoveries seem too wacky to be true. Can you uncover the weird truth from these facts? Keep track of your answers on a separate sheet of paper.

"THE FACTS"

	TRUE	FALSE
1. The microwave was invented when a chocolate bar melted in a scientist's pocket.	☐	☐
2. A vengeful scientist tried to destroy the world's computers with the Y2K virus.	☐	☐
3. Penicillin was discovered by accident.	☐	☐
4. One of the 20th century's biggest scientific discoveries was an elaborate hoax.	☐	☐
5. When the Hubble Telescope was first launched, it didn't work.	☐	☐
6. When a low-tack glue was invented, at first no one could think of a use for it.	☐	☐
7. Scientists have reproduced the Big Bang in a lab.	☐	☐

1. THE MICROWAVE WAS INVENTED WHEN A CHOCOLATE BAR MELTED IN A SCIENTIST'S POCKET.

TRUE

In 1946 scientist Percy Spencer was checking a piece of equipment called a magnetron, which is the power tube in a radar machine. As he stood in front of it, a bar of chocolate in his pocket began to melt. Later he asked for a bag of corn kernels and held it near the magnetron. His hunch was right—the kernels exploded into puffy white popcorn! From this experiment the microwave oven was born.

[image: Popcorn Scientists]

2. A VENGEFUL SCIENTIST TRIED TO DESTROY THE WORLD'S COMPUTERS WITH THE Y2K VIRUS.

FALSE

The Y2K bug was a glitch in computer programs, where the first two digits of the year were fixed at "19." This wasn't a problem until scientists realized that at midnight on December 31, 1999, the computers would return to 1900. People feared that the bug would cause computer failures and chaos. The programs were rewritten, and the year 2000 arrived without mishap.

3. PENICILLIN WAS DISCOVERED BY ACCIDENT.

TRUE

A substance called penicillin is one of medicine's most important discoveries, but it was actually found by accident. In 1928 scientist Alexander Fleming noticed that a bacterial culture growing in a Petri dish in his lab was contaminated with mold. Around the mold there was no bacteria. Thankfully, Fleming decided to investigate. His discovery led to the birth of penicillin, the world's first antibiotic, which has saved countless lives.

4. ONE OF THE 20TH CENTURY'S BIGGEST SCIENTIFIC DISCOVERIES WAS AN ELABORATE HOAX.

TRUE

In 1912 a skull was unearthed in Piltdown, England. Scientists were very excited by the find, since it seemed to be the skull of an early human. The fact that it was found next to what seemed to be a prehistoric cricket bat should have aroused suspicion, but it wasn't until 1953 that it was proved to be an elaborate hoax. An ape's jaw had been attached to a human skull, then aged with chemicals.

5. WHEN THE HUBBLE TELESCOPE WAS FIRST LAUNCHED, IT DIDN'T WORK.

TRUE

The Hubble Telescope was launched in 1990. It cost $2 billion to make, but the first pictures it sent back were useless. Investigations discovered that the curve of the telescope's huge mirror was off by less than a fiftieth of the width of a human hair. As a result, the pictures it produced were blurred. During a daring spacewalk, astronauts attached mirrors to fix it, allowing Hubble to send back incredible images of the universe.

6. WHEN A LOW-TACK GLUE WAS INVENTED, AT FIRST NO ONE COULD THINK OF A USE FOR IT.

TRUE

When Stephen Silver invented a not-very-sticky peel able glue, he couldn't think of a use for it and felt like a failure. Luckily, his colleague, Art Fry, suggested using it on small strips of paper as a place marker in a book, and in 1980 the Post-it note was born.

7. SCIENTISTS HAVE REPRODUCED THE BIG BANG IN A LAB.

FALSE

The Big Bang is the name given to events that occurred during the early development of the universe. The Large Hadron Collider (LHC) tries to re-create the conditions that existed shortly after the Big Bang rather than the moment itself. It isn't kept in a traditional science lab; the LHC is enormous. It is housed in a circular tunnel that runs for 16.5 miles (27 km) under Switzerland.

Chapter Four

CURIOUS CURES

QUIZ In the past, many weird and wacky medical practices were common. Examine the facts below and give your diagnosis. Write your answers on a separate sheet of paper..

THE "FACTS"

	TRUE	FALSE
1. In the Stone Age some illnesses were "cured" by drilling a hole in the patient's skull.	☐	☐
2. Today no one believes that people get sick because of evil spirits.	☐	☐
3. Maggots and leeches help healing.	☐	☐
4. Medieval barbers performed surgery and dentistry.	☐	☐
5. In the past, operations were performed without reliable pain relief.	☐	☐
6. In times of plague, doctors wore bird masks.	☐	☐

1. IN THE STONE AGE SOME ILLNESSES WERE "CURED" BY DRILLING A HOLE IN THE PATIENT'S SKULL.

TRUE

"Trepanning" was a form of Stone Age surgery where a hole was drilled with a flint chisel into the head of an unfortunate patient. Scientists can't be certain, but they think that it may have been done to let out what people then believed to be "evil spirits" trapped in the brain of a person who was mentally ill, or possibly to cure a headache before painkillers were developed.

2. TODAY NO ONE BELIEVES THAT PEOPLE GET SICK BECAUSE OF EVIL SPIRITS.

FALSE

Doctors have accepted for a long time that most illnesses are caused by bacteria and viruses, not evil spirits. However, in some parts of the world, people still believe that some illnesses are caused by evil spirits attacking the person. In the Voodoo religion, the idea of spirit and healing is central. If spirits are not respected, people believe they will cause problems.

3. MAGGOTS AND LEECHES HELP HEALING.

TRUE

You may be surprised to hear that maggots and leeches still play a part in medicine today. Maggots have been used for hundreds of years as a method of cleaning wounds. They eat only dead or rotting tissue, leaving healthy flesh untouched, so they are great for helping wounds heal. Leeches were used originally to suck out "bad blood," and although there's no scientific basis for this, they do produce a chemical that prevents blood from clotting. Applying leeches to a wound site increases the blood flow to the area, which aids recovery. The only thing patients have to overcome is the yuck factor!

4. MEDIEVAL BARBERS PERFORMED SURGERY AND DENTISTRY.

TRUE

The red-and-white pole outside a barber's shop symbolizes bloodletting, one of the many medical procedures barbers used to perform. In 1540 things began to change, and a law was passed that decreed that British barbers must not carry out any kind of surgery, apart from pulling teeth.

5. IN THE PAST, OPERATIONS WERE PERFORMED WITHOUT RELIABLE PAIN RELIEF.

TRUE

Before 1846, patients undergoing operations suffered dreadful agony. They often died from shock or infection after surgery, and the only way to minimize suffering was to operate as quickly as possible while the patient was held down. In 1846 a substance called ether was used by Robert Liston. Patients slept and felt no pain. Chloroform was subsequently used, but it was better hygiene that really increased a patient's chances of recovery.

6. IN TIMES OF PLAGUE, DOCTORS WORE BIRD MASKS.

TRUE

Plague wiped out millions of people during epidemics. The worst was the Black Death, which struck several times during the 14th century and killed more than 25 million people in Europe alone. During times of plague, people known as "plague doctors" wore terrifying bird masks with hollow beaks stuffed full of herbs and flowers. They believed that these would protect the wearer from catching the disease. The masks also protected them from the terrible smell of the plague victims.

INGENIOUS INVENTIONS

QUIZ

There are millions of brilliant gadgets that make life a little easier, but some inventions are so crazy they can't be real—or can they? Try to spot the fakes from the facts. Keep score on a separte sheet of paper.

THE "FACTS"

	TRUE	FALSE
1. In Japan a toilet for fish has been developed.	☐	☐
2. You can make ice cream by rolling a ball around.	☐	☐
3. You can buy removable tattoo sleeves.	☐	☐
4. The Uno is a one-wheeled motorcycle.	☐	☐
5. Doggles are sunglasses for dogs.	☐	☐
6. The Japanese word *chindogu* means "most useful invention."	☐	☐

1. IN JAPAN A TOILET FOR FISH HAS BEEN DEVELOPED.

FALSE

There's no such thing as a toilet for fish, but there is a toilet with a built-in fish tank. The transparent cistern was designed in China for people who don't have much room for pets. It is perfectly safe for the fish, since the aquarium water in which they swim is in a separate tank.

2. YOU CAN MAKE ICE CREAM BY THROWING A BALL AROUND.

TRUE

What could be nicer than a little exercise followed by some ice cream? It's easy with a special plastic ball. You pour yummy ingredients, plus some ice and salt, into the spaces inside the ball. Throw and catch the ball for 20 minutes until your chilly treat is ready to enjoy.

3. YOU CAN BUY REMOVABLE TATTOO SLEEVES.

TRUE

If you're too young for a tattoo, or if you're old enough and always wanted one but are too scared of the pain, try fake tattoo sleeves. The flesh-colored nylon sleeves come decorated with a selection of designs. The cuffs can be covered up with bracelets or watches. Best of all, if you get tired of them, you can take them off!

4. THE UNO IS A ONE-WHEELED MOTORCYCLE.

FALSE

At first glance the Uno looks like a unicycle crossed with a motorcycle, with one wheel. Actually, it has two wheels that sit side by side. The flick of a switch can transform it into a traditional motorcycle.

6. DOGGLES ARE SUNGLASSES FOR DOGS.

TRUE

It's the latest "must have" doggy fashion item. These doggy sunglasses don't mist up, don't let in insects or flies, and provide protection from the sun's dangerous rays.
[image: doggles]

5. THE JAPANESE WORD *CHINDOGU* MEANS "MOST USEFUL INVENTION."

FALSE

While many of the world's most bizarre inventions come from Japan, *chindogu* refers to the process of inventing an everyday gadget that solves a problem, but in turn is so embarrassing or tricky to use that it is almost useless. Examples of chindogu include mini umbrellas to be worn on the toes of your shoes and a hay fever hat—essentially a toilet roll dispenser worn on your head.

EXOTIC EXPLORERS

QUIZ

Over the years, explorers have embarked on intrepid travels to find uncharted territory. But can you pick out the traveling truths? See if you were heading in the right direction or totally lost. Keep a record of your answers on a separate shet of paper.

THE "FACTS"

	TRUE	FALSE
1. Captain Cook died in Hawaii.	☐	☐
2. The first explorer to reach the South Pole was Robert Falcon Scott.	☐	☐
3. Sir Walter Raleigh tried to colonize America	☐	☐
4. A Viking explorer reached North America 500 years before Columbus.	☐	☐
5. The first attempt to conquer Mount Everest was made in 1953.	☐	☐
6. In South America, Spanish explorers found El Dorado, the lost city of gold.	☐	☐

1. CAPTAIN COOK DIED IN HAWAII.

TRUE

In the 18th century, Captain Cook made three daring voyages, during which he saw many countries that were new to Europeans, including Australia, New Zealand, and the coast of Antarctica. In 1779 he set sail on his third voyage and reached Hawaii. At first Cook and his crew were welcomed, but after a while, there was friction with the islanders, which ultimately led to Cook's being stabbed to death.

2. THE FIRST EXPLORER TO REACH THE SOUTH POLE WAS ROBERT FALCON SCOTT.

FALSE

In 1912, when Robert Falcon Scott made a grueling trek to the South Pole, he found himself in a race with a team of Norwegians, led by Roald Amundsen. Both men were determined to reach the Pole first. When Scott's team finally reached their target, to their dismay they found the Norwegians had beaten them to it—by a month. On the return journey, Scott and his team perished from starvation and frostbite.

3. SIR WALTER RALEIGH TRIED TO COLONIZE AMERICA.

TRUE

Sir Walter Raleigh is one of England's best-known explorers. In the 16th century, England's queen, Elizabeth I, granted Raleigh permission to colonize America to make England more powerful and wealthy. Raleigh provided financial backing for the first voyage in 1585, and a colony was established at Roanoke Island in what's now North Carolina. It was very short-lived. The settlers were poorly equipped and returned to Britain in 1586.

4. A VIKING EXPLORER REACHED NORTH AMERICA 500 YEARS BEFORE COLUMBUS.

TRUE

Around the year 1000, Leif Eriksson, son of the Viking warrior Erik the Red, was blown off course while sailing from Greenland to Norway. Stories refer to him arriving in a place he called Vinland. There is evidence of a Viking settlement in what is now Newfoundland, Canada, which matches descriptions of Vinland, so it appears Columbus may have been 500 years too late!

5. THE FIRST ATTEMPT TO CONQUER MOUNT EVEREST WAS MADE IN 1953.

FALSE

The imposing peak called Mount Everest lies in a mountain range known as the Himalayas. Seven expeditions to climb to the summit, the first in 1922, were unsuccessful. In 1953, when Sir Edmund Hillary and his Sherpa mountain guide, Tenzing Norgay, set out to conquer Everest, no one was sure if it was possible. Hillary and Norgay spent hours battling the bad weather and ferocious winds that whip across the mountain. When they reached the top, Hillary famously said that they could see "the whole world spread out below us."

6. IN SOUTH AMERICA, SPANISH EXPLORERS FOUND EL DORADO, THE LOST CITY OF GOLD.

FALSE

When Spanish explorers heard tales of a mythical lost city made of gold, they were determined to find the place known as El Dorado. Many searched, but it was never found. This legend probably arose from stories of a tribal ceremony. A new king would be covered in gold, making him a "gilded man" or "El Dorado." It's possible these stories were exaggerated over time to become the legend of a city of gold.

Chapter Seven

MAN–MADE MADNESS

QUIZ Some of the things humans have created are really amazing, while others are just plain crazy. Can you tell which of these facts are true and which are utter nonsense? Mark your answers on a separate sheet of paper.

THE "FACTS"

	TRUE	FALSE
1. In Florida, divers can stay in a hotel 21 feet (6 m) under water.	☐	☐
2. Diamonds can be grown in a lab.	☐	☐
3. In Holland there is a museum located inside a human body.	☐	☐
4. In the 1940s the American military developed a flying saucer.	☐	☐
5. In Dubai a star-shaped island has been built.	☐	☐
6. Scientists have successfully created artificial life.	☐	☐

1. IN FLORIDA, DIVERS CAN STAY IN A HOTEL 21 FEET (6 M) UNDER WATER.

TRUE

Jules's Undersea Lodge in Florida rests 21 feet (6 m) below the surface, at the bottom of a lagoon. Guests scuba dive down to the entrance and step into the lodge through a small, open pool in the wet room. There, they can have a shower and dry off, then relax in the living spaces. Compressed air is pumped into the lodge to stop it from filling with water. There's a living room, bedrooms, and huge round windows through which guests can watch the underwater wildlife.

2. DIAMONDS CAN BE GROWN IN A LAB.

TRUE

Scientists first discovered how to grow, or "culture," synthetic diamonds in the 1950s. Since then, technological advances have led to labs growing diamonds to sell for jewelry and other purposes. Cultured diamonds are real in the sense that they are made of carbon, just like natural diamonds that take millions of years to form. The difference is that cultured diamonds can be grown in just a few days.

3. IN HOLLAND THERE IS A MUSEUM LOCATED INSIDE A HUMAN BODY.

FALSE

You won't find the Corpus Museum in Holland inside a real human body. However, it is built inside a giant replica of the human body. Inside, visitors take an interactive journey though the body. You can be a red blood cell, step inside a mouth, and even poke around in a replica of the brain.

4. IN THE 1940s THE AMERICAN MILITARY DEVELOPED A FLYING SAUCER.

FALSE

It wasn't a flying saucer; it was an experimental plane that looked a little like one, designed by Charles Zimmerman, an aeronautical engineer. Although it had a saucerlike shape, it still had wings and propellers. The idea was that it would fly at great speeds and be able to make short landings on aircraft carriers. The US Navy was so impressed that two prototypes were built. However, with the arrival of the jet engine, propeller planes became less popular and the project was abandoned. You could say that the idea never really took off!

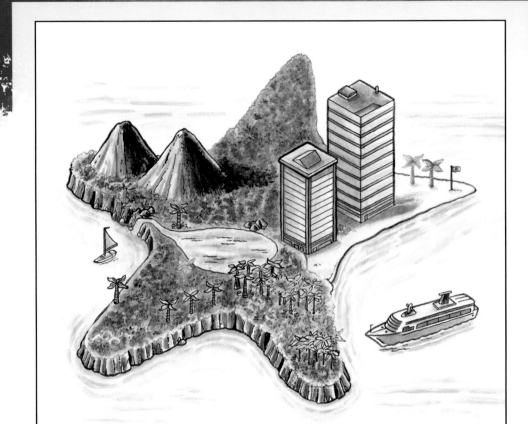

5. IN DUBAI A STAR-SHAPED ISLAND HAS BEEN BUILT.

FALSE

While it is true that three man-made islands have been constructed in Dubai, they are in the shape of three giant palms, not stars. The islands are called Jumeirah, Jebel Ali, and Deira. Jumeirah is home to an expensive hotel and luxury apartments, as well as restaurants, shops, and leisure facilities.

6. SCIENTISTS HAVE SUCCESSFULLY CREATED ARTIFICIAL LIFE.

TRUE

In a laboratory in Maryland, Dr. Craig Venter became the first biologist to create artificial life. He constructed a bacteria from new DNA. It is based on an existing bacteria but uses genetic information constructed in the laboratory. It has been named Synthia, because of its synthetic origin, and its DNA contains a special watermark to show that it is artificial.

YOUR SCORE

On a separate piece of paper, copy this chart and add up your scores for each section. There are 44 in total. Count every correct answer as one. Then find the grand total. The higher your number, the better you are at detecting the truth!

Terrific Technology	
Dramatic Discoveries	
Weird Science	
Curious Cures	
Ingenious Inventions	
Exotic Explorers	
Man-Made Madness	
TOTAL	

aeronautics—The science or study of travel through the air.

antibiotics—Medicine (such as penicillin) that inhibits the growth of harmful bacteria or other microorganisms.

astronomer—Someone who studies the stars.

colonize—To send a group of settlers to an area to establish control over it.

electromagnet—Soft metal made into a magnet by the passing of an electrical current through it.

expedition—A journey undertaken by a group of people to serve a specific purpose such as exploration, colonization, or research.

heresy—A belief or opinion opposing those held by mainstream religions.

magnetron—An electron tube for amplifying or generating microwaves.

FURTHER READING

BOOKS

Farndon, John. *Exploring Science: Inventions & Discoveries*. Hacheote, TX: Armadillo Publishing, 2016.

Goldsmith, Mike. *Eureka!: The Most Amazing Scientific Discoveries of All Time.* New York, NY: Thames and Hudson Publishing, 2014.

Ruzicka, Oldrich, and Silvie Sanza. *Time Traveler Inventions: Travel Through Time and Take a Peek into the World of Scientific & Technological Inventions*, Minneapolis, MN: Walter Foster Jr. Publications, 2015.

Williams, Rachel. *Atlas of Adventures: A Collection of Natural Wonders, Exciting Experiences, and Fun Festivities From the Four Corners of the Globe.* New York, NY: Wide Eyed Editions, 2015.

Zourelias, Diana. *Fun Facts About Everyday Inventions.* Mineola, NY: Dover Publications, 2013.

WEBSITES

www.timeforkids.com/homework-helper/study-helper/famous-inventors
Short biographies of famous inventors from around the world!

kidskonnect.com/science/inventors-inventions/
Fast facts about inventors and inventions.

cybersleuth-kids.com/sleuth/Science/Inventors/
More facts about science and inventions!